Living and Working in Colonial Times™

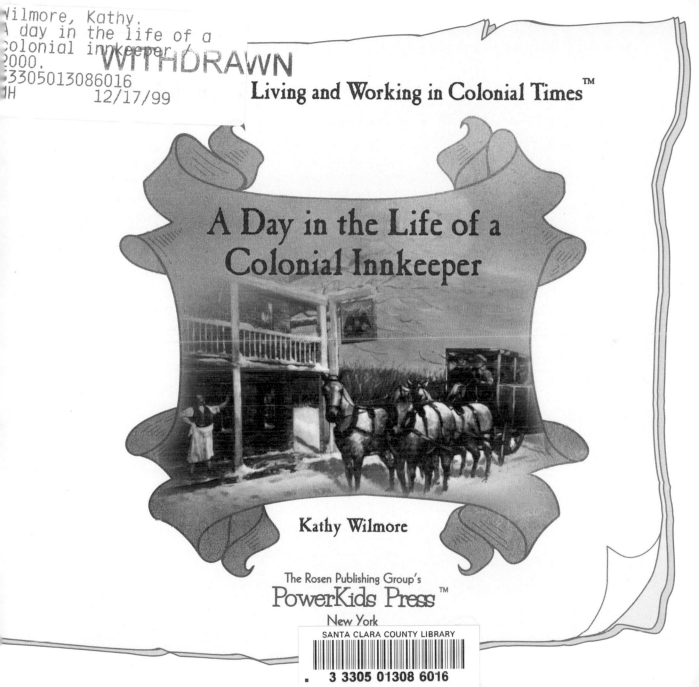

A Day in the Life of a Colonial Innkeeper

Kathy Wilmore

The Rosen Publishing Group's
PowerKids Press™
New York

To Bryan Brown, for the encouragement, humor, and grace that helped so much as I
wrote this book—and to my mother, Julia C. Wilmore, who got me started.

Published in 2000 by The Rosen Publishing Group, Inc.
29 East 21st Street, New York, NY 10010

First Edition

Book design: Danielle Primiceri

Photo Credits: Cover, pp. 1, 16, 19 © The Granger Collection, New York; p. 4 © CORBIS/Bettmann; pp. 7,
20 © North Wind Picture Archives; pp. 8, 11 © CORBIS; p. 12 © SuperStock; p. 15 © Joe Viesti/Viesti
Associates, Inc.

Wilmore, Kathy.
    A day in the life of a colonial innkeeper / Kathy Wilmore.
        p.   cm. — (The library of living and working in colonial times)
    Includes index.
    Summary: Describes the life of a colonial Massachusetts innkeeper, including his daily work, the rules he
had to follow, and life in his town.
    ISBN 0-8239-5430-7 (lib. bdg.)
    1. Hotelkeepers—Juvenile literature. [1. Food industry and trade—History.] I. Title. II. Series.
TX910.3.W55 1998
647.94744'01'09032—dc21
                                                                                                    98-49396
                                                                                                       CIP
                                                                                                        AC

Manufactured in the United States of America

Jacob Watkins, his family, and their inn are fictional, but the details in this story about Colonial inns and
Colonial life are true.

Contents

Colonial America

On July 4, 1776, the United States of America became an **independent** country. For almost 170 years before that, the thirteen original states were **colonies** of England. That period in American history, from about 1607 until 1776, is called Colonial America.

Most **colonists** came here from Europe. As time passed, they began to feel more American than European. They came up with more and more **traditions** and lifestyles all their own.

◀ *Grateful Pilgrims arrive in America in 1620.*

The Red Lion Inn

A young man named Isaac Watkins sailed to America from England in 1652. He built a large house in **rural** Massachusetts.

Travelers who came through town had no place to stay. People let them sleep in their homes or barns. Isaac Watkins and his family enjoyed having travelers stay with them. In 1660, a new Massachusetts law required every town to have a place for travelers to stay. Isaac Watkins turned his home into an **inn**. He called it the Red Lion.

This innkeeper welcomes a tired traveler. ▶

Early to Rise

Many years later, Isaac's inn was still in business. His great-grandson, Jacob Watkins, and his wife, Lila, ran the place. Innkeepers like Mr. and Mrs. Watkins woke before sunrise every day and went to work. Mrs. Watkins started a fire in the kitchen, for cooking and cleaning. Nellie, the maid, fed the chickens and milked the cow. Mr. Watkins built a fire in the dining room, so guests who came down to breakfast would be warm. Ezra, the stable boy, fed and watered the guests' horses.

◀ *This woman prepares dinner at the fire for her guests.*

Sending Them Off

Mr. and Mrs. Watkins and the servants hurried through their breakfast. Soon, while it was still dark, the first guests came downstairs. Mrs. Watkins and Nellie served them breakfast. It was hot corn-mush, boiled ham, and coffee.

Mr. Watkins found out when each guest would leave. Then Ezra brought each traveler's horse or carriage to the front of the inn. If a guest needed help, Mr. Watkins drew a map or gave directions.

This innkeeper and his family live and work at their inn. ▶

Comings and Goings

Several carriages a day arrived from faraway places. Some passengers came to visit relatives and friends. Others came to do business. Ezra, the stable boy, fed and watered the horses, while the drivers and passengers rested at the inn. Mr. Watkins gave the tired travelers food, or a fire to relax by. Soon, they were off again.

Small Colonial towns had no post offices, so drivers often left mail at the inn. Townsfolk stopped by to see if anything had come for them.

◀ *Colonial travelers arrive at an inn.*

In Town and at Home

Mrs. Watkins sent Nellie to pick vegetables from the garden. Then Mrs. Watkins walked to the butcher shop to buy meat. She and Nellie had a lot of meals to cook for the hungry guests at the inn. Mrs. Watkins and Nellie also swept and tidied up the guest **chambers**.

According to an old English tradition, each guest bedroom at an inn had its own name. The Red Lion's bedrooms had names like the Red Rose Chamber, the Sun Chamber, and the North Star Room.

A Colonial bedchamber. ▶

By the Rules

Innkeepers in Colonial Massachusetts had to have a **license** to run an inn. Sometimes a **magistrate** stopped by to make sure that Jacob Watkins was obeying the rules. Laws required inns to have large, easy-to-spot signs. A sign had to be easy to understand, even for travelers who could not read.

The law told Mr. Watkins how much he could charge for beds, food, and drink. For example, one law said that innkeepers could charge no more than **sixpence** for a meal.

◀ *An inn's sign was a welcome sight for Colonial travelers.*

Welcome to The Red Lion!

As evening fell, most travelers decided to stay for the night. There were very few good roads beyond the cities and towns, so it could be hard to find one's way in the dark. It could also be dangerous, if bandits were about.

Mrs. Watkins made a stew of boiled meat and vegetables for dinner, which Mr. Watkins served to the guests. Nellie heated bricks to put under the guests' bedcovers. That left a nice, toasty spot for bedtime. Ezra got the horses settled for the night.

These guests at a Colonial inn rest by a warm fire and wait for dessert. ▶

Talk of the Town

Inns like Jacob Watkins's were the only places in small Colonial towns where people could gather in the evenings. Most of the talk was about England's King George and his high **taxes**. People **debated** whether the colonies should fight for independence from England. This would mean the colonies would be free to rule themselves.

The lion and the color red were symbols of England, so Mr. Watkins decided to rename The Red Lion. He called it the Blue Eagle Inn.

◀ *These men enjoy talking at a Colonial inn*

Late to Bed

The innkeepers stayed up until the last traveler went to bed. Jacob Watkins gathered shoes from outside each guest's door. He cleaned them, then put them back by the doors. Mrs. Watkins mixed batter for the next day's bread. They put out the fires and piled firewood for morning. Finally, they put out their candles and went to sleep. Soon it would be morning, with another busy day's work ahead.

Web Sites:

http://www.colonialwilliamsburg.org
http://www.history.org/life/life.htm

Glossary

chamber (CHAYM-bur) A room; usually a bedroom.

colonist (KAH-luh-nist) A person who lives in a colony.

colony (KAH-luh-nee) An area in a new country where a large group of people move, but they are still ruled by the leaders and laws of their old country.

debate (dih-BAYT) To argue or discuss.

independent (in-dih-PEN-dint) Being able to think and do things for oneself.

inn (IN) A place, like a hotel, where travelers can get food and a bed to sleep in while they are away from home.

license (LY-sints) Official permission to do something.

magistrate (MA-jih-STRAYT) An official whose job is to make sure laws are obeyed.

rural (RUR-ul) In the country or in a farming area.

sixpence (SIKS-pents) A coin that was worth six pennies.

taxes (TAK-sez) Money that people give the government to help pay for public services.

traditions (truh-DIH-shunz) Ways of doing things that are important to people, and that a group of people have usually done the same way for a long time.

Index